To:

_____

From:

_____

Date:

_____

Promises from God's Heart: Comforting Truth for Your Every Need
© 2018 DaySpring Cards, Inc. All rights reserved.

First Edition, November 2018

Published by:

DaySpring

P.O. Box 1010
Siloam Springs, AR 72761
dayspring.com

Compiled by Lisa Stilwell
Designed by Greg Jackson of thinkpen.design
Printed in China

Prime:
71923 Classic
71924 Feminine
71928 Contemporary

ISBN:
978-1-68408-214-8 Classic
978-1-68408-215-5 Feminine
978-1-68408-219-3 Contemporary

Promises
FROM God's
Heart

COMFORTING TRUTH FOR
YOUR EVERY NEED

CONTENTS

6

Introduction

"I promise!"

These two words are so simple, yet they are filled with power and anticipation of something binding and strong. We hear and say them from the time we're born, and use them to ensure that our word is true. Parents promise to be there for us, friends promise to be our best friend forever, and as we get older, a fiancé promises to be "yours til death do us part." But as we grow, it doesn't take long to realize that not everyone keeps his or her promises—and with every broken promise falls a broken piece of heart. When that happens, how do you know who to believe and trust anymore?

Well, there is One who can always be trusted—He's got a perfect record for keeping promises. God and His Word are full of assurances that have remained true and reliable since the beginning of time. Just as He promised prophets and disciples from the Old and New Testaments, He hears your every prayer today and vows to give you hope that you can believe in. If you are trying to overcome fear, He promises to give you His strength. If you are hurting, He will give comfort and fill you with peace. There are hundreds of them filled with His commitment of love and faithfulness, provision and grace, and so much more.

No matter where you are in life or what circumstance you find yourself, He's made pledges straight from His heart to yours to help you throughout each day and every need of your journey. Read them, memorize them, and know with full confidence that you are loved and cared for with the greatest capacity ever known to humankind. Those are just a few of God's promises to you.

> For all God's words are right,
> and everything he does is
> worthy of our trust.
>
> Psalm 33:4 TLB

Just think,
You're here not by chance,
but by God's choosing.
His hand formed you
and made you the person you are.
He compares you to no one else—
you are one of a kind.
You lack nothing
that His grace can't give you.
He has allowed you to be here
at this time in history
to fulfill His special purpose
for this generation.

—Roy Lessin

To every thing there is a season,
and a time to every purpose
under the heaven.

Ecclesiastes 3:1 KJV

PROMISES *from* GOD'S HEART
WHEN YOU ARE *afraid*...

God is our refuge and strength,
a helper who is always found
in times of trouble.
Therefore we will not be afraid.

—*Psalm 46:1-2*

The Lord is my light and my salvation—
whom shall I fear?
The Lord is the stronghold of my life—
of whom shall I be afraid?

—*Psalm 27:1 NIV*

There is no fear in love; instead, perfect love drives
out fear, because fear involves punishment. So the
one who fears has not reached perfection in love.

—*1 John 4:18*

Fear not, for I am with you;
be not dismayed, for I am your God;
I will strengthen you, I will help you,
I will uphold you with my righteous right hand.
—*Isaiah 41:10* ESV

In my distress I called to the L ord;
I called out to my God.
From his temple he heard my voice;
my cry came to his ears.
—*2 Samuel 22:7* NIV

For you did not receive the spirit of
slavery to fall back into fear, but you
have received the Spirit of adoption as
sons, by whom we cry, "Abba! Father!"
—*Romans 8:15* ESV

> We have this hope as an anchor
> for our lives, safe and secure.
> —*Hebrews 6:19*

For You have been a stronghold for the poor,
a stronghold for the needy person in his distress,
a refuge from the rain, a shade from the heat.
—*Isaiah 25:4*

But whoever listens to me will live securely
and be free from the fear of danger.
—*Proverbs 1:33*

PROMISES *from* GOD'S HEART
WHEN YOU ARE *angry* ...

Don't hit back; discover beauty in everyone.
If you've got it in you, get along with everybody.
Don't insist on getting even; that's not for you to do.
"I'll do the judging," says God. "I'll take care of it."
—*Romans* 12:19 THE MESSAGE

For if you forgive people their wrongdoing,
your heavenly Father will forgive you as well.
—*Matthew* 6:14

Refrain from anger and give up
your rage; do not be agitated—
it can only bring harm.
—*Psalm* 37:8

Stop being mean, bad-tempered, and angry.
Quarreling, harsh words, and dislike of others
should have no place in your lives. Instead, be
kind to each other, tenderhearted, forgiving
one another, just as God has forgiven
you because you belong to Christ.

—*Ephesians 4:31–32* TLB

A gentle answer turns away anger,
but a harsh word stirs up wrath.

—*Proverbs 15:1*

Refrain from anger
and turn from wrath;
do not fret—
it leads only to evil.
—*Psalm 37:8* NIV

Be completely humble and gentle; be patient,
bearing with one another in love. Make every
effort to keep the unity of the Spirit through the
bond of peace. . . . to each one of us grace has
been given as Christ apportioned it.

—*Ephesians 4:3–4, 7 NIV*

Sing to Yahweh, you His faithful ones,
and praise His holy name.
For His anger lasts only a moment,
but His favor, a lifetime.
Weeping may spend the night,
but there is joy in the morning.

—*Psalm 30:4–6*

PROMISES *from* GOD'S HEART
WHEN YOU ARE *anxious*...

Don't worry about anything, but in everything,
through prayer and petition with thanksgiving,
let your requests be made known to God. And
the peace of God, which surpasses every thought,
will guard your hearts and minds in Christ Jesus.

—*Philippians 4:6*

Those who know your name trust in
you, for you, LORD, have never
forsaken those who seek you.

—*Psalm 9:10 NIV*

Don't have so little faith! Don't always think about
what you will eat or what you will drink. Don't worry
about it. All the people in the world are trying to get
those things. Your Father knows that you need them.

—*Luke 12:28–30 ICB*

> Remember, your Father knows exactly
> what you need even before you ask him!
> —*Matthew 6:8* TLB

Trust in the Lord with all your heart,
and do not rely on your own understanding;
think about Him in all your ways,
and He will guide you on the right paths.
—*Proverbs 3:5–6*

Seek first his kingdom and his righteousness,
and all these things will be given to you as
well. Therefore do not worry about tomorrow,
for tomorrow will worry about itself. Each
day has enough trouble of its own.
—*Matthew 6:32–34* NIV

> Be still before the LORD
> and wait patiently for him.
> —*Psalm 37:7*

Humble yourselves, therefore, under God's mighty hand, that he may lift you up in due time. Cast all your anxiety on him because he cares for you.

—*1 Peter 5:6 NIV*

Cast your burden on the LORD,
and He will sustain you;
He will never allow the
righteous to be shaken.

—*Psalm 55:22*

Promises *from* God's heart for *comfort*...

Blessed are those who mourn,
for they shall be comforted.
—*Matthew 5:4* ESV

The LORD is near the brokenhearted;
He saves those crushed in spirit.
—*Psalm 34:18*

Praise the God and Father of our Lord Jesus Christ,
the Father of mercies and the God of all comfort.
He comforts us in all our affliction, so that we may
be able to comfort those who are in any kind of
affliction, through the comfort we ourselves receive
from God. For as the sufferings of Christ overflow
to us, so through Christ our comfort also overflows.
—*2 Corinthians 1:3–5*

Even though I walk through the darkest
valley, I will fear no evil, for you are with me;
your rod and your staff, they comfort me.

—*Psalm 23:4 NIV*

The LORD gives His people strength;
the LORD blesses His people with peace.

—*Psalm 29:11*

Because of the LORD's gracious love
we are not consumed,
since his compassions never end.
They are new every morning.

—*Lamentations 3:22–23 ISV*

Why, my soul, are you downcast?
Why so disturbed within me?
Put your hope in God,
for I will yet praise him,
my Savior and my God.

—*Psalm 42:5*

He tends his flock like a shepherd:
He gathers the lambs in his arms
and carries them close to his heart.

—*Isaiah 40:11 NIV*

God—He clothes me with strength
and makes my way perfect.
He makes my feet like the feet of a deer
and sets me securely on the heights.

—*Psalm 18:32–33*

PROMISES *from* GOD'S HEART
WHEN YOU ARE *confused*...

Trust in the LORD with all your heart
and lean not on your own understanding;
in all your ways submit to him,
and he will make your paths straight.
—*Proverbs 3:5–6 NIV*

> For God is not a God
> of confusion but of peace.
> —*1 Corinthians 14:33 NASB*

Now if any of you lacks wisdom, he should ask God, who gives to all generously and without criticizing, and it will be given to him.

—*James 1:5*

The one who gets wisdom loves life; the one who cherishes understanding will soon prosper.

—*Proverbs 19:8 NIV*

Now we have this treasure in clay jars, so that this extraordinary power may be from God and not from us. We are pressured in every way but not crushed; we are perplexed but not in despair; we are persecuted but not abandoned; we are struck down but not destroyed.

—*2 Corinthians 4:7–9*

> All the Lord's ways show faithful
> love and truth to those who keep
> His covenant and decrees.
> —*Psalm 25:10*

Obey the laws of God and follow all his
ways; keep each of his commands written in
the law of Moses so that you will prosper in
everything you do, wherever you turn.
—*1 Kings 2:3* TLB

Now this is our boast: Our conscience testifies that
we have conducted ourselves in the world, and
especially in our relations with you, with integrity
and godly sincerity. We have done so, relying
not on worldly wisdom but on God's grace.
—*2 Corinthians 1:12* NIV

Promises *from* God's heart for *courage* ...

> Immediately Jesus spoke to them.
> "Have courage! It is I. Don't be afraid."
> —*Matthew* 14:27

"I repeat, be strong and brave! Don't be afraid and don't panic, for I, the LORD your God, am with you in all you do."
—*Joshua* 1:9 NET

But Christ, God's faithful Son, is in complete charge of God's house. And we Christians are God's house—he lives in us!—if we keep up our courage firm to the end, and our joy and our trust in the Lord.
—*Hebrews* 3:6 TLB

"I have told you these things so that in Me you may
have peace. You will have suffering in this world.
Be courageous! I have conquered the world."
—*John 16:33*

Wait on the LORD;
Be of good courage,
And He shall strengthen your heart;
Wait, I say, on the LORD!
—*Psalm 27:14* NKJV

"For I am the LORD your God who
takes hold of your right hand and says
to you, Do not fear; I will help you."
—*Isaiah 41:13* NIV

You have clothed me with strength for battle;
You subdue my adversaries beneath me.
—*Psalm 18:39*

In Him we have boldness and confident
access through faith in Him.
—*Ephesians 3:12*

This High Priest of ours understands our
weaknesses, for he faced all of the same testings
we do, yet he did not sin. So let us come boldly
to the throne of our gracious God. There
we will receive his mercy, and we will find
grace to help us when we need it most.
—*Hebrews 4:15–16* NLT

Promises *from* God's heart when you are *depressed*...

Why are you in despair, O my soul?
Why have you become restless and disquieted
within me? Hope in God and wait expectantly
for Him, for I shall yet praise Him, The help
of my countenance and my God.

—*Psalm 42:11* AMP

If your heart is broken, you'll find God right
there; if you're kicked in the gut, he'll
help you catch your breath.

—*Psalm 34:18* THE MESSAGE

He heals the brokenhearted
and binds up their wounds.

—*Psalm 147:3* ESV

The Spirit of the Lord God . . .
has sent Me to heal the brokenhearted . . .
to comfort all who mourn, to provide for those
who mourn in Zion; to give them a crown of
beauty instead of ashes, festive oil instead
of mourning, and splendid clothes instead
of despair. And they will be called righteous
trees, planted by the LORD to glorify Him.
—*Isaiah 61:1–3*

In my distress I called to the LORD,
and He answered me.
—*Psalm 120:1*

Always be full of joy in the Lord; I say it
again, rejoice! . . . Remember that the Lord is coming
soon. Don't worry about anything; instead, pray
about everything; tell God your needs . . . If you
do this, you will experience God's peace . . . His
peace will keep your thoughts and your hearts
quiet and at rest as you trust in Christ Jesus.

—*Philippians 4:4–7* TLB

Sing to Yahweh, you His faithful ones,
and praise His holy name.
For His anger lasts only a moment,
but His favor, a lifetime.
Weeping may spend the night,
but there is joy in the morning.

—*Psalm 30:4–5*

PROMISES *from* GOD'S HEART FOR WHEN YOU ARE *discouraged*...

Have I not commanded you? Be strong
and courageous. Do not be afraid; do not
be discouraged, for the LORD your God
will be with you wherever you go.

—*Joshua 1:9 NIV*

A man who endures trials is blessed, because when
he passes the test he will receive the crown of life
that God has promised to those who love Him.

—*James 1:12*

You will succeed if you carefully follow the
statutes and ordinances the LORD commanded
Moses for Israel. Be strong and courageous.
Don't be afraid or discouraged.

—*1 Chronicles 22:13*

Why, my soul, are you downcast?
Why so disturbed within me?
Put your hope in God,
for I will yet praise him,
my Savior and my God.

—*Psalm 42:11 NIV*

Take My yoke upon you and learn from
Me, for I am gentle and lowly in heart,
and you will find rest for your souls.

—*Matthew 11:29 NKJV*

But as for you, be strong; don't be
discouraged, for your work has a reward.

—*2 Chronicles 15:7*

> I have said these things to you, that in me you may have peace. In the world you will have tribulation. But take heart; I have overcome the world.
>
> —*John 16:33 ESV*

I can do all this through him who gives me strength.
—*Philippians 4:13 NIV*

The LORD is the One who will go before you. He will be with you; He will not leave you or forsake you. Do not be afraid or discouraged.
—*Deuteronomy 31:8*

Promises *from* God's heart when you have *doubt*...

But when [Peter] saw the strength of the wind,
he was afraid. And beginning to sink he cried out,
"Lord, save me!" Immediately Jesus reached out His
hand, caught hold of him, and said to him,
"You of little faith, why did you doubt?" When
they got into the boat, the wind ceased.

—*Matthew 14:30–32*

> "Truly, I say to you, whoever says
> to this mountain, 'Be taken up and
> thrown into the sea,' and does not
> doubt in his heart, but believes
> that what he says will come to
> pass, it will be done for him."
>
> —*Mark 11:23 ESV*

If you want to know what God wants you to do, ask him, and he will gladly tell you, for he is always ready to give a bountiful supply of wisdom to all who ask him; he will not resent it. But when you ask him, be sure that you really expect him to tell you, for a doubtful mind will be as unsettled as a wave of the sea that is driven and tossed by the wind; and every decision you then make will be uncertain, as you turn first this way and then that. If you don't ask with faith, don't expect the Lord to give you any solid answer.

—*James 1:5–8* TLB

Jesus answered them, "I assure you: If you have faith and do not doubt, you will not only do what was done to the fig tree, but even if you tell this mountain, 'Be lifted up and thrown into the sea,' it will be done. And if you believe, you will receive whatever you ask for in prayer."

—*Matthew 21:21–22*

He commanded us to preach to the people and to testify that he is the one whom God appointed as judge of the living and the dead. All the prophets testify about him that everyone who believes in him receives forgiveness of sins through his name.

—*Acts 10:42–43 NIV*

PROMISES *from* GOD'S HEART
FOR *encouragement*…

Do not fear, for I am with you;
do not be afraid, for I am your God.
I will strengthen you; I will help you;
I will hold on to you with My righteous right hand.

—*Isaiah 41:10*

God, hear my cry;
pay attention to my prayer.
I call to You from the ends of the earth
when my heart is without strength.
Lead me to a rock that is high above me,
for You have been a refuge for me,
a strong tower in the face of the enemy.

—*Psalm 61:1–3*

> When we obey him, every path he guides us on is fragrant with his loving-kindness and his truth.
>
> —*Psalm 25:10*

For I am sure that neither death nor life, nor angels nor rulers, nor things present nor things to come, nor powers, nor height nor depth, nor anything else in all creation, will be able to separate us from the love of God in Christ Jesus our Lord.

—*Romans 8:38–39 ESV*

There is no one like the God of Jeshurun,
who rides across the heavens to help you
and on the clouds in his majesty.
The eternal God is your refuge,
and underneath are the everlasting arms.

—*Deuteronomy 33:26–27 NIV*

What a wonderful God we have—he is the
Father of our Lord Jesus Christ, the source of
every mercy, and the one who so wonderfully
comforts and strengthens us in our hardships
and trials. And why does he do this? So that
when others are troubled, needing our sympathy
and encouragement, we can pass on to them
this same help and comfort God has given us.

—*2 Corinthians 1:3–4*

"This is what the LORD says, he who
made the earth, the LORD who formed
it and established it—the LORD is
his name: 'Call to me and I will
answer you and tell you great and
unsearchable things you do not know.'"

—*Jeremiah 33:2–3 NIV*

Promises *from* God's heart for *endurance*...

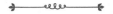

I call to God;
God will help me.
At dusk, dawn, and noon I sigh
deep sighs—he hears, he rescues.
My life is well and whole, secure . . .
—*Psalm 55:16–17* THE MESSAGE

> So we must not get tired of doing good, for we will reap at the proper time if we don't give up.
> —*Galatians 6:9*

The Lord is my rock, and my safe place, and the
One Who takes me out of trouble. My God is my
rock, in Whom I am safe. He is my safe-covering,
my saving strength, and my strong tower.

—*Psalm 18:2* NLV

> He gives strength to the weary
> and strengthens the powerless.
> —*Isaiah 40:29*

And not only that, but we also rejoice in our
afflictions, because we know that affliction
produces endurance, endurance produces
proven character, and proven character produces
hope. This hope will not disappoint us, because
God's love has been poured out in our hearts
through the Holy Spirit who was given to us.

—*Romans 5:3–5* CSB

We continually ask God to fill you with the knowledge of his will through all the wisdom and understanding that the Spirit gives, so that you may live a life worthy of the Lord and please him in every way: bearing fruit in every good work, growing in the knowledge of God, being strengthened with all power according to his glorious might so that you may have great endurance and patience, and giving joyful thanks to the Father, who has qualified you to share in the inheritance of his holy people in the kingdom of light.

—*Colossians 1:9–12 NIV*

Splendor and majesty are before him; strength and joy are in his dwelling place.

—*1 Chronicles 16:27 NIV*

PROMISES *from* GOD'S HEART
FOR *eternal life...*

For God loved the world in this way: He gave His
One and Only Son, so that everyone who believes
in Him will not perish but have eternal life.

—*John 3:16*

> But he was pierced for
> our transgressions, he was crushed
> for our iniquities; the punishment
> that brought us peace was on him,
> and by his wounds we are healed.
>
> —*Isaiah 53:5 NIV*

I tell you the truth, whoever hears what I say
and believes in the One who sent me has eternal
life. That person will not be judged guilty but
has already left death and entered life.

—*John 5:24 NCV*

For we know that if our temporary, earthly dwelling is destroyed, we have a building from God, an eternal dwelling in the heavens, not made with hands.

—*2 Corinthians 5:1*

Because you will not abandon me to the realm of the dead, nor will you let your faithful one see decay. You make known to me the path of life; you will fill me with joy in your presence, with eternal pleasures at your right hand.

—*Psalm 16:10–11 NIV*

> How great are His miracles, and how
> mighty His wonders! His kingdom is
> an eternal kingdom, and His dominion
> is from generation to generation.
> —*Daniel 4:3*

Yet God has made everything beautiful for its
own time. He has planted eternity in the human
heart, but even so, people cannot see the whole
scope of God's work from beginning to end.
—*Ecclesiastes 3:11* NLT

And this is the testimony: God has given
us eternal life, and this life is in His Son.
The one who has the Son has life.
—*1 John 5:11–12*

Promises *from* God's heart for His *favor*...

For You, Lord, bless the righteous one; You
surround him with favor like a shield.
—*Psalm 5:12*

How blessed is God! And what a blessing he is!
He's the Father of our Master, Jesus Christ, and
takes us to the high places of blessing in him.
Long before he laid down earth's foundations, he
had us in mind, had settled on us as the focus of
his love, to be made whole and holy by his love.
—*Ephesians 1:5–6 THE MESSAGE*

For what credit is it if you sin and
are mistreated and endure it? But
if you do good and suffer and so
endure, this finds favor with God.
—*1 Peter 2:20 NET*

Sing the praises of the LORD,
you his faithful people;
praise his holy name.
For his anger lasts only a moment,
but his favor lasts a lifetime;
weeping may stay for the night,
but rejoicing comes in the morning.

—*Psalm 30:4–5* NIV

My hand made all these things, and so
they all came into being. This is the Lord's
declaration. I will look favorably on this kind
of person: one who is humble, submissive
in spirit, and trembles at My word.

—*Isaiah 66:2*

Suddenly a great company of the heavenly host
appeared with the angel, praising God and saying,
"Glory to God in the highest heaven,
and on earth peace to those on whom his favor rests."
—*Luke 2:13–14 NIV*

Blessings on all who reverence and
trust the Lord—on all who obey him!
Their reward shall be prosperity and
happiness. . . . That is God's reward to
those who reverence and trust him.

—*Psalm 128:1–2, 4 TLB*

PROMISES *from* GOD'S HEART
WHEN YOU ARE *faithful*...

Blessings on you if I return and find you faithfully
doing your work. I will put such faithful ones
in charge of everything I own!
—*Matthew 24:46–47* TLB

The loving-kindness of the Lord is from everlasting
to everlasting to those who reverence him; his
salvation is to children's children of those who are
faithful to his covenant and remember to obey him!
—*Psalm 103:17–18* TLB

Lying lips are detestable to the Lord,
but faithful people are His delight.
—*Proverbs 12:22*

I am grateful to the one who has strengthened
me, Christ Jesus our Lord, because he considered
me faithful in putting me into ministry . . .

—*1 Timothy 1:12* NET

His master said to him, "Well done, good and faithful
servant. You have been faithful and trustworthy
over a little, I will put you in charge of many
things; share in the joy of your master."

—*Matthew 25:23* AMP

Loyalty and faithfulness
deliver a king; through loyalty
he maintains his throne.

—*Proverbs 20:28*

> In every situation take the
> shield of faith, and with it you
> will be able to extinguish all the
> flaming arrows of the evil one.
> —*Ephesians 6:16*

Know therefore that the Lord your God is
God; he is the faithful God, keeping his covenant
of love to a thousand generations of those who
love him and keep his commandments.

—*Deuteronomy 7:9* NIV

Know that the Lord has set apart
the faithful for Himself;
the Lord will hear when I call to Him.

—*Psalm 4:3*

Promises *from* God's heart regarding *forgiveness* ...

> We have redemption,
> the forgiveness of sins, in Him.
> —*Colossians 1:14*

If you, God, kept records on wrongdoings,
  who would stand a chance?
As it turns out, forgiveness is your habit,
  and that's why you're worshiped.
I pray to God—my life a prayer—
  and wait for what he'll say and do.
My life's on the line before God, my Lord,
  waiting and watching till morning . . .

  —*Psalm 130:3–6 THE MESSAGE*

[Jesus] took a cup, gave thanks, and gave it to [the disciples], saying, "Drink from this, all of you. This is my blood of the covenant, which is poured out for many so that their sins may be forgiven.

—*Matthew 26:27–28* CEV

"Do not judge, and you will not be judged. Do not condemn, and you will not be condemned. Forgive, and you will be forgiven."

—*Luke 6:37*

Blessed and happy and favored are those whose lawless acts have been forgiven, and whose sins have been covered up and completely buried.

—*Romans 4:7* AMP

Anyone who speaks a word against the Son of Man will be forgiven, but anyone who speaks against the Holy Spirit will not be forgiven, either in this age or in the age to come.

—*Matthew 12:32* NIV

If you forgive anyone, I [Paul] do too. For what I have forgiven—if I have forgiven anything—it is for you in the presence of Christ. I have done this so that we may not be taken advantage of by Satan. For we are not ignorant of his schemes.

—*2 Corinthians 2:10–11*

We have redemption in Him through His blood, the forgiveness of our trespasses, according to the riches of His grace that He lavished on us with all wisdom and understanding.

—*Ephesians 1:7–8*

PROMISES *from* GOD'S HEART
FOR HIS *friendship* ...

> Friendship with God is reserved
> for those who reverence him.
> With them alone he shares the
> secrets of his promises.
>
> —*Psalm* 25:14 TLB

He guarantees right up to the end that you will
be counted free from all sin and guilt on that
day when he returns. God will surely do this for
you, for he always does just what he says, and he
is the one who invited you into this wonderful
friendship with his Son, even Christ our Lord.

—*1 Corinthians* 1:8–9

When I think of You as I lie on my bed,
I meditate on You during the night watches
because You are my helper;
I will rejoice in the shadow of Your wings.
I follow close to You;
Your right hand holds on to me.
—*Psalm 63:6–8*

On one of those days while [Jesus] was teaching
. . . some men came, carrying on a mat a man
who was paralyzed. . . . Seeing their faith He
said, "Friend, your sins are forgiven you."
—*Luke 5:17, 18, 20*

You make known to me the path
of life; you will fill me with joy
in your presence, with eternal
pleasures at your right hand.
—*Psalm 16:11 NIV*

> For David said this about him: "I keep the Lord before me always. Because he is close by my side, I will not be hurt."
>
> —*Acts 2:25 NCV*

How happy is the one You choose
and bring near to live in Your courts!
We will be satisfied with the
goodness of Your house,
the holiness of Your temple.

—*Psalm 65:4*

PROMISES *from* GOD'S HEART FOR YOUR *future* . . .

> For I know the plans I have for you,"
> declares the LORD, "plans to prosper
> you and not to harm you, plans
> to give you hope and a future."
> —*Jeremiah 29:11 NIV*

LORD, you are my portion
and my cup of blessing;
you hold my future.
The boundary lines have fallen for me
in pleasant places;
indeed, I have a beautiful inheritance.
—*Psalm 16:5–6 CSB*

> Don't be envious of sinful people;
> let reverence for the LORD be
> the concern of your life. If it is,
> you have a bright future.
> —*Proverbs 23:17–18* GNT

Keep your voice from weeping
and your eyes from tears,
for the reward for your work will come—
this is the LORD's declaration . . .
There is hope for your future—
this is the LORD's declaration.
—*Jeremiah 31:16–17*

Honey whets the appetite and so does wisdom!
When you enjoy becoming wise, there is
hope for you! A bright future lies ahead!
—*Proverbs 24:14* TLB

Come now, you who say, "Today or tomorrow we will travel to such and such a city and spend a year there and do business and make a profit." You don't even know what tomorrow will bring— what your life will be! For you are like smoke that appears for a little while, then vanishes. Instead, you should say, "If the Lord wills, we will live and do this or that."

—*James 4:13–15*

Ask me, and I will make the nations your inheritance, the ends of the earth your possession.
—*Psalm 2:8 NIV*

PROMISES *from* GOD'S HEART
WHEN YOU *give*...

> "Give, and it will be given to you;
> a good measure—pressed down,
> shaken together, and running
> over—will be poured into your lap.
> For with the measure you use, it
> will be measured back to you."
> —*Luke 6:38*

"So whenever you give to the poor, don't sound
a trumpet before you, as the hypocrites do in the
synagogues and on the streets, to be applauded by
people. I assure you: They've got their reward! But
when you give to the poor, don't let your left
hand know what your right hand is doing, so
that your giving may be in secret. And your
Father who sees in secret will reward you."
—*Matthew 6:2–4*

> "And anyone who gives one of my most humble followers a cup of cool water, just because that person is my follower, will surely be rewarded."
> —*Matthew* 10:42 CEV

A poor widow came and put in two small copper coins, which make a penny. And he called his disciples to him and said to them, "Truly, I say to you, this poor widow has put in more than all those who are contributing to the offering box. For they all contributed out of their abundance, but she out of her poverty has put in everything she had, all she had to live on."

—*Mark* 12:42–44 ESV

"Bring the whole tithe into the storehouse, that there may be food in my house. Test me in this," says the LORD Almighty, "and see if I will not throw open the floodgates of heaven and pour out so much blessing that there will not be room enough to store it."

—*Malachi 3:9–10 NIV*

But remember this—if you give little, you will get little. A farmer who plants just a few seeds will get only a small crop, but if he plants much, he will reap much. Everyone must make up his own mind as to how much he should give. Don't force anyone to give more than he really wants to, for cheerful givers are the ones God prizes.

—*2 Corinthians 9:6–7 TLB*

PROMISES *from* GOD'S HEART
FOR HIS *grace* ...

For you are saved by grace through faith, and
this is not from yourselves; it is God's gift—
not from works, so that no one can boast.
—*Ephesians 2:8–9*

For the LORD God is a sun and shield;
The LORD bestows grace and favor and honor;
No good thing will He withhold from
those who walk uprightly.
—*Psalm 84:11 AMP*

The LORD laughs at those who
laugh at him, but he gives grace
to those who are not proud.
—*Proverbs 3:34 NCV*

The Word became flesh and took up
residence among us. We observed His glory,
the glory as the One and Only Son from
the Father, full of grace and truth.
Indeed, we have all received grace after grace from
His fullness, for the law was given through Moses,
grace and truth came through Jesus Christ.

—*John 1:14*

For you are saved by grace through
faith, and this is not from
yourselves; it is God's gift.

—*Ephesians 2:8*

> God resists the proud,
> but gives grace to the humble.
> —*James 4:6*

"My grace is sufficient for you, for power is perfected in weakness." Therefore, I [Paul] will most gladly boast all the more about my weaknesses, so that Christ's power may reside in me.

—*2 Corinthians 12:1*

Now I [Luke] commit you to God and to the word of his grace, which can build you up and give you an inheritance among all those who are sanctified.

—*Acts 20:32 NIV*

PROMISES *from* GOD'S HEART IN TIMES OF *grief*...

────◆────

> The LORD is close to the brokenhearted,
> and he saves those whose
> spirits have been crushed.
> —*Psalm 34:18 NCV*

What a wonderful God we have—he is the
Father of our Lord Jesus Christ, the source of
every mercy, and the one who so wonderfully
comforts and strengthens us in our hardships
and trials. And why does he do this? So that
when others are troubled, needing our sympathy
and encouragement, we can pass on to them
this same help and comfort God has given us.

—*2 Corinthians 1:4 TLB*

Deep calls to deep in the roar of Your waterfalls;
all Your breakers and Your billows
have swept over me.
The LORD will send His faithful love by day;
His song will be with me in the night—
a prayer to the God of my life.

—*Psalm 42:7–8*

"But I will send you the Comforter—the Holy
Spirit, the source of all truth. He will come to you
from the Father and will tell you all about me."

—*John 15:26 TLB*

Because of the LORD's great
love we are not consumed, for
his compassions never fail.

—*Lamentations 3:22 NIV*

May our Lord Jesus Christ Himself and God
our Father, who has loved us and given us
eternal encouragement and good hope by
grace, encourage your hearts and strengthen
you in every good work and word.

—*2 Thessalonians 2:16–17*

Look! God's dwelling is with humanity,
and He will live with them.
They will be His people,
and God Himself will be with them
and be their God.
He will wipe away every tear from their eyes.
Death will no longer exist;
grief, crying, and pain will exist no longer,
because the previous things have passed away.

—*Revelation 21:3–4*

PROMISES *from* GOD'S HEART FOR HIS *guidance* ...

When the Spirit of truth comes, He will guide you into all the truth. For He will not speak on His own, but He will speak whatever He hears. He will also declare to you what is to come.

—*John 16:13*

Trust in the LORD with all your heart, and do not rely on your own understanding; think about Him in all your ways, and He will guide you on the right paths.

—*Proverbs 3:5–6*

I will lead the blind along an unfamiliar
way; I will guide them down paths
they have never traveled. I will
turn the darkness in front of them
into light, and level out the rough
ground. This is what I will do for
them. I will not abandon them.

—*Isaiah 42:16* NET

Be strong and courageous, for you will distribute
the land I swore to their fathers to give them
as an inheritance. Above all, be strong and
very courageous to carefully observe the whole
instruction My servant Moses commanded
you. Do not turn from it to the right or the left,
so that you will have success wherever you go.

—*Joshua 1:6–7*

How happy is the man who does not follow the
advice of the wicked or take the path of
sinners or join a group of mockers! Instead,
his delight is in the LORD's instruction,
and he meditates on it day and night.

—*Psalm 1:1–2*

Do not conform to the pattern of this world, but
be transformed by the renewing of your mind.
Then you will be able to test and approve what
God's will is—his good, pleasing and perfect will.

—*Romans 12:2 NIV*

Be careful to do as the LORD your God has
commanded you; you are not to turn aside
to the right or the left. Follow the whole
instruction the LORD your God has commanded
you, so that you may live, prosper, and have
a long life in the land you will possess.

—*Deuteronomy 5:32–33*

PROMISES *from* GOD'S HEART FOR *healing*...

> He heals the brokenhearted
> and binds up their wounds.
> —*Psalm 147:3*

Do not be wise in your own eyes;
Fear the LORD and turn away from evil.
It will be healing to your body
And refreshment to your bones.
—*Proverbs 3:7–8* NASB

Those who hope in the LORD will renew their
strength. They will soar on wings like
eagles; they will run and not grow weary,
they will walk and not be faint.
—*Isaiah 40:31* NIV

But [Jesus] was pierced because of our
transgressions, crushed because of our
iniquities; punishment for our peace was on
Him, and we are healed by His wounds.

—*Isaiah 53:5*

My roots will have access to water,
and the dew will rest on my branches all night.
My strength will be refreshed within me,
and my bow will be renewed in my hand.

—*Job 29:19–20*

If my people will humble themselves and pray,
and search for me, and turn from their wicked
ways, I will hear them from heaven and forgive
their sins and heal their land. I will listen, wide
awake, to every prayer made in this place.

—*2 Chronicles 7:14–15*

> Therefore we do not give up.
> Even though our outer person is
> being destroyed, our inner person
> is being renewed day by day.
> —*2 Corinthians 4:16*

In your unfailing love you will lead
the people you have redeemed.
In your strength you will guide them
to your holy dwelling.
—*Exodus 15:13* NIV

Promises *from* God's heart for the hope of *heaven*...

> For we know that if our temporary,
> earthly dwelling is destroyed,
> we have a building from God,
> an eternal dwelling in the
> heavens, not made with hands.
>
> —*2 Corinthians 5:1*

Praise be to the God and Father of our Lord
Jesus Christ! In his great mercy he has given
us new birth into a living hope through the
resurrection of Jesus Christ from the dead, and
into an inheritance that can never perish, spoil or
fade. This inheritance is kept in heaven for you.

—*1 Peter 1:3–4 NIV*

For God so loved the world in this way: He gave His One and Only Son, so that everyone who believes in Him will not perish but have eternal life.

—*John 3:16*

Whoever practices and teaches these commands will be called great in the kingdom of heaven.

—*Matthew 5:19*

"I am the living bread that came down from heaven. If anyone eats of this bread he will live forever. The bread that I will give for the life of the world is My flesh."

—*John 6:51*

You are saved by grace! Together with Christ Jesus He also raised us up and seated us in the heavens, so that in the coming ages He might display the immeasurable riches of His grace through His kindness to us in Christ Jesus.

—*Ephesians 2:5–7*

Our citizenship is in heaven, from which we also eagerly wait for a Savior, the Lord Jesus Christ. He will transform the body of our humble condition into the likeness of His glorious body, by the power that enables Him to subject everything to Himself.

—*Philippians 3:20–21*

Promises *from* God's heart for *His return...*

> "But I tell you, in the future you will see the Son of Man seated at the right hand of the Power and coming on the clouds of heaven."
>
> —*Matthew 26:64*

Now concerning how and when all this will happen, dear brothers and sisters, we don't really need to write you. For you know quite well that the day of the Lord's return will come unexpectedly, like a thief in the night.

—*1 Thessalonians 5:1–2 NLT*

[Jesus] said to [some of the disciples], "Are you asking one another about what I said, 'A little while and you will not see Me; again a little while and you will see Me'? "I assure you: You will weep and wail, but the world will rejoice. You will become sorrowful, but your sorrow will turn to joy. When a woman is in labor she has pain because her time has come. But when she has given birth to a child, she no longer remembers the suffering because of the joy that a person has been born into the world. So you also have sorrow[d] now. But I will see you again. Your hearts will rejoice, and no one will rob you of your joy. In that day you will not ask Me anything.

—*John 16:19–23*

> For the Son of Man is going to come with His angels in the glory of His Father, and then He will reward each according to what he has done.
>
> —*Matthew 16:27*

For the Lord himself will come down from heaven, with a loud command, with the voice of the archangel and with the trumpet call of God, and the dead in Christ will rise first. After that, we who are still alive and are left will be caught up together with them in the clouds to meet the Lord in the air. And so we will be with the Lord forever.

—*1 Thessalonians 4:16–17 NIV*

PROMISES *from* GOD'S HEART
REGARDING THE *Holy Spirit* ...

And I will ask the Father, and He will give you
another Counselor to be with you forever. He
is the Spirit of truth. The world is unable to
receive Him because it doesn't see Him or
know Him. But you do know Him, because
He remains with you and will be in you.

—*John 14:16–18*

John [the Baptist] answered them
all, "I baptize you with water,
but One is coming who is more
powerful than I. . . . He will baptize
you with the Holy Spirit . . ."

—*Luke 3:15–16*

Turn to me and receive my gentle correction; Watch and I will pour out my spirit on you; I will share with you my wise words in order to redirect your lives.

—*Proverbs 1:23* VOICE

I will give you a new heart and put a new spirit within you; I will remove your heart of stone and give you a heart of flesh. I will place My Spirit within you and cause you to follow My statutes and carefully observe My ordinances.

—*Ezekiel 36:26–27*

Also, the Spirit helps us with our weakness. We do not know how to pray as we should. But the Spirit himself speaks to God for us, even begs God for us with deep feelings that words cannot explain. God can see what is in people's hearts. And he knows what is in the mind of the Spirit, because the Spirit speaks to God for his people in the way God wants.

—*Romans 8:26–27* NCV

Whoever speaks a word against the Son of Man, it will be forgiven him. But whoever speaks against the Holy Spirit, it will not be forgiven him, either in this age or in the one to come.

—*Matthew 12:32*

The one who keeps His commands remains in Him, and He in him. And the way we know that He remains in us is from the Spirit He has given us.

—*1 John 3:24*

It is true that I baptise you with water as a sign of your repentance, but the one who follows me is far stronger than I am—indeed I am not fit to carry his shoes. He will baptise you with the fire of the Holy Spirit.

—*Matthew 3:11 PHILLIPS*

Promises *from* God's heart
when you need *hope*...

Love the Lord, all His faithful ones.
The Lord protects the loyal,
but fully repays the arrogant.
Be strong and courageous,
all you who put your hope in the Lord.
—*Psalm 31:23–24*

Don't envy sinners,
but always continue to fear the Lord.
You will be rewarded for this;
your hope will not be disappointed.
—*Proverbs 23:17–18 NLT*

A man's steps are established by the Lord,
and He takes pleasure in his way.
Though he falls, he will not be overwhelmed,
because the Lord holds his hand.
—*Psalm 37:23–24*

For I know the plans I have for you," declares the LORD, "plans to prosper you and not to harm you, plans to give you hope and a future.

—*Jeremiah 29:11 NIV*

Because of the LORD's faithful love
we do not perish,
for His mercies never end.
They are new every morning;
great is Your faithfulness!
I say: The LORD is my portion,
therefore I will put my hope in Him.

—*Lamentations 3:22–24*

> Therefore, since we have been declared righteous by faith, we have peace with God through our Lord Jesus Christ. We have also obtained access through Him by faith into this grace in which we stand, and we rejoice in the hope of the glory of God.
>
> —*Romans 5:1–2*

But now he has reconciled you by Christ's physical body through death to present you holy in his sight, without blemish and free from accusation—if you continue in your faith, established and firm, and do not move from the hope held out in the gospel.

—*Colossians 1:22–23 NIV*

PROMISES *from* GOD'S
HEART FOR HIS *joy* ...

You will show me the path of life;
In Your presence is fullness of joy;
In Your right hand there are pleasures forevermore.
—*Psalm 16:11 AMP*

What happiness for those whose guilt
has been forgiven! What joys when
sins are covered over! What relief for
those who have confessed their sins
and God has cleared their record.
—*Psalm 32:2 TLB*

If you keep My commands you will remain
in My love, just as I have kept My Father's
commands and remain in His love.
"I have spoken these things to you so that My joy
may be in you and your joy may be complete.
—*John 15:10–11*

His glorious power will make you
patient and strong enough to endure
anything, and you will be truly happy.
—*Colossians 1:11 CEV*

You love him even though you have never seen him;
though not seeing him, you trust him; and even
now you are happy with the inexpressible joy that
comes from heaven itself. And your further reward
for trusting him will be the salvation of your souls.

—*1 Peter 1:8–9* TLB

You turned my lament into dancing;
You removed my sackcloth
and clothed me with gladness,
so that I can sing to You and not be silent.
LORD my God, I will praise You forever.

—*Psalm 30:11–12*

Now may the God of hope fill you
with all joy and peace as you believe
in Him so that you may overflow with
hope by the power of the Holy Spirit.

—*Romans 15:13*

PROMISES *from* GOD'S HEART FOR *justice* . . .

> Your throne is founded on two strong pillars—the one is Justice and the other Righteousness. Mercy and Truth walk before you as your attendants.
> —*Psalm 89:14 TLB*

Then the Lord said . . . "Will not God grant justice to His elect who cry out to Him day and night? Will He delay to help them? I tell you that He will swiftly grant them justice."
—*Luke 18:6–8*

The works of His hands are truth and justice;
all His instructions are trustworthy.
They are established forever and ever,
enacted in truth and in what is right.
—*Psalm 11:7–8*

True justice must be given to foreigners
living among you and to orphans,
and you must never accept a widow's
garment as security for her debt.

—*Deuteronomy 24:17* NLT

Here is My Servant whom I have chosen,
My beloved in whom My soul delights;
I will put My Spirit on Him,
and He will proclaim justice to the nations.

—*Matthew 12:28*

But the LORD sits enthroned forever;
He has established His throne for judgment.
He judges the world with righteousness;
He executes judgment on the nations with fairness.
The LORD is a refuge for the oppressed,
a refuge in times of trouble.

—Psalm 9:7–9

The God of Israel spoke;
the Rock of Israel said to me:
"Whoever rules fairly over people,
who rules with respect for God,
is like the morning light at dawn,
like a morning without clouds.
He is like sunshine after a rain
that makes the grass sprout
from the ground."

—2 Samuel 23:3–4 NCV

PROMISES *from* GOD'S HEART
WHEN YOU ARE *lonely*...

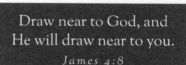

Draw near to God, and
He will draw near to you.

James 4:8

The LORD is my shepherd;
there is nothing I lack.
He lets me lie down in green pastures;
He leads me beside quiet waters.
He renews my life;
He leads me along the right paths
for His name's sake.
Even when I go through the darkest valley,
I fear no danger,
for You are with me;
Your rod and Your staff—they comfort me.

—Psalm 23:1–4

> Call on me and come and pray to me, and I will listen to you. You will seek me and find me when you seek me with all your heart.
> —*Jeremiah 29:12–13 NIV*

For I am persuaded that not even death or life, angels or rulers, things present or things to come, hostile powers, height or depth, or any other created thing will have the power to separate us from the love of God that is in Christ Jesus our Lord!

—*Romans 8:38–39*

> God has said: "I will never leave you nor forsake you".
> —*Hebrews 13:5* PHILLIPS

Praise the God and Father of our Lord Jesus Christ, the Father of mercies and the God of all comfort. He comforts us in all our affliction, so that we may be able to comfort those who are in any kind of affliction, through the comfort we ourselves receive from God.

—*2 Corinthians 1:3–4*

The Lord is fair in everything he does and full of kindness. He is close to all who call on him sincerely. He fulfills the desires of those who reverence and trust him; he hears their cries for help and rescues them.

—*Psalm 145:17–19* TLB

PROMISES *from* GOD'S HEART
FOR HIS STEADFAST *love* . . .

All the paths of the LORD lead to
gracious love and truth for those who
keep his covenant and his decrees.

—*Psalm 25:10 ISV*

"Though the mountains move
and the hills shake,
My love will not be removed from you
and My covenant of peace will not be shaken,"
says your compassionate LORD.

—*Isaiah 54:10*

> For God so loved the world that he gave his one and only Son, that whoever believes in him shall not perish but have eternal life.
>
> —*John 3:16 NIV*

"The one who has My commands and keeps them is the one who loves Me. And the one who loves Me will be loved by My Father. I also will love him and will reveal Myself to him."

—*John 14:21*

But when the kindness of God our Savior and His love for mankind appeared, He saved us—not by works of righteousness that we had done, but according to His mercy, through the washing of regeneration and renewal by the Holy Spirit.

—*Titus 3:4–5*

Now may our Lord Jesus Christ himself,
and God our Father, who loved us and gave
us eternal comfort and good hope through
grace, comfort your hearts and establish
them in every good work and word.

—*2 Thessalonians 2:16–17*

> LORD, your love reaches to the heavens,
> your loyalty to the skies.
>
> —*Psalm 36:5 NCV*

Promises *from* God's heart for His *mercy* ...

> The Lord is very
> compassionate and merciful.
> —*James 5:11*

But as for me, I will sing each morning
about your power and mercy. For you
have been my high tower of refuge, a
place of safety in the day of my distress.
—*Psalm 59:16* TLB

For we do not have a high priest incapable of
sympathizing with our weaknesses, but one who
has been tempted in every way just as we are,
yet without sin. Therefore let us confidently
approach the throne of grace to receive mercy
and find grace whenever we need help.

—*Hebrews 4:15–16* NET

What a contrast between Adam and Christ
who was yet to come! And what a difference
between man's sin and God's forgiveness!
For this one man, Adam, brought death to many
through his sin. But this one man, Jesus Christ,
brought forgiveness to many through God's mercy.

—*Romans 5:14–15* TLB

Praise be to the LORD,
for he has heard my cry for mercy.
The LORD is my strength and my shield;
my heart trusts in him, and he helps me.
—*Psalm 28:6–7* NIV

He who conceals his transgressions
will not prosper, but whoever
confesses and turns away from his
sins will find compassion and mercy.
—*Proverbs 28:13* AMP

PROMISES *from* GOD'S HEART REGARDING *money* . . .

> Wealth gained quickly will dwindle
> away, but the one who gathers it
> little by little will become rich.
> —*Proverbs 13:11 NET*

Honor the LORD with your wealth
and with the best part of everything you produce.
Then he will fill your barns with grain,
and your vats will overflow with good wine.

—*Proverbs 3:9–10 NLT*

Whenever you give to the poor, don't sound a trumpet before you, as the hypocrites do in the synagogues and on the streets, to be applauded by people. I assure you: They've got their reward! But when you give to the poor, don't let your left hand know what your right hand is doing, so that your giving may be in secret. And your Father who sees in secret will reward you.

—*Matthew 6:2–4*

Evil men borrow, but do not repay their debt, but the godly show compassion and are generous.

—*Psalm 37:21* NET

Why do you spend money on what is not food,
and your wages on what does not satisfy?
Listen carefully to Me, and eat what is good,
and you will enjoy the choicest of foods.
Pay attention and come to Me;
listen, so that you will live.
I will make an everlasting covenant with you,
the promises assured to David.

—*Isaiah 55:2–3*

Your life should be free from the love of money. Be satisfied with what you have, for He Himself has said, I will never leave you or forsake you.

—*Hebrews 13:5*

PROMISES *from* GOD'S HEART
WHEN YOU ARE *obedient*...

But those who teach God's laws and obey
them shall be great in the Kingdom of Heaven.
—*Matthew 5:19* TLB

For the LORD gives wisdom;
from His mouth come knowledge
and understanding.
He stores up success for the upright;
He is a shield for those who live with integrity
so that He may guard the paths of justice
and protect the way of His loyal followers.
—*Proverbs 2:6–8*

"If you follow My statutes and faithfully observe
My commands, I will give you rain at the right
time, and the land will yield its produce, and
the trees of the field will bear their fruit."

—*Leviticus 26:3–4*

If only you had obeyed my commandments,
prosperity would have flowed to you like
a river, deliverance would have come
to you like the waves of the sea.
—*Isaiah 48:18* NET

> The one who keeps His commands
> remains in Him, and He in him. And
> the way we know that He remains in
> us is from the Spirit He has given us.
> —*1 John 3:24*

Obey me, and I will be your God and you shall be
my people; only do as I say, and all shall be well!
—*Jeremiah 7:23* TLB

"Though your sins are like scarlet,
they will be as white as snow;
though they are as red as crimson,
they will be like wool.
If you are willing and obedient,
you will eat the good things of the land."
—*Isaiah 1:18–19*

For You, LORD, bless the righteous one;
You surround him with
favor like a shield.
—*Psalm 5:12*

PROMISES *from* GOD'S HEART
WHEN YOU ARE FEELING
overwhelmed...

A man's steps are established by the LORD,
and He takes pleasure in his way.
Though he falls, he will not be overwhelmed,
because the LORD holds his hand.

—*Psalm 37:23–24*

You who answer prayer,
to you all people will come.
When we were overwhelmed by sins,
you forgave our transgressions.
Blessed are those you choose
and bring near to live in your courts!

—*Psalm 65:2–4 NIV*

> "Come to Me, all of you who are weary and burdened, and I will give you rest."
> —*Matthew 11:28*

God is our refuge and strength, a helper who is always found in times of trouble.
—*Psalm 46:1*

The God of all grace, who has called you to his eternal glory in Christ, will himself restore, confirm, strengthen, and establish you . . .
—*1 Peter 5:10 ESV*

But You, Lord, are a shield around me, my glory, and the One who lifts up my head.

—*Psalm 3:3*

Cast your burden on the LORD—
he will support you!
God will never let the
righteous be shaken!

—*Psalm 55:22* CEB

Promises *from* God's heart
when you need *peace*...

> The LORD gives His people strength;
> the LORD blesses His people with peace.
>
> —*Psalm 29:11*

Don't worry about anything; instead, pray about
everything; tell God your needs, and don't forget
to thank him for his answers. If you do this, you
will experience God's peace, which is far more
wonderful than the human mind can understand.
His peace will keep your thoughts and your hearts
quiet and at rest as you trust in Christ Jesus.

—*Philippians 4:6–7 TLB*

Let the peace that comes from Christ rule in your hearts. For as members of one body you are called to live in peace. And always be thankful.

—*Colossians* 3:15 NLT

But the fruit of the Spirit is love, joy, peace, patience, kindness, goodness, faithfulness, gentleness, and self-control.

—*Galatians* 5:22 CEB

Abundant peace belongs to those who love Your instruction; nothing makes them stumble.

—*Psalm* 119:165

"Peace I leave with you. My peace I give you. I give to you not as the world gives. Don't be troubled or afraid."
—*John 14:27* CEB

You have put more joy in my heart
than they have when their grain
and new wine abound.
I will both lie down and sleep in peace,
for You alone, Lᴏʀᴅ, make me live in safety.
—*Psalm 4:7–8*

PROMISES *from* GOD'S HEART
FOR HIS *power* ...

"You will receive power when the Holy
Spirit has come on you . . ."
—*Acts 1:8*

Ascribe power to God.
His majesty is over Israel,
His power among the clouds.
God, You are awe-inspiring in Your sanctuaries.
The God of Israel gives power and strength
to His people. May God be praised!
—*Psalm 68:34–35*

Fan into flame the gift of God, which is in you
through the laying on of my hands. For the
Spirit God gave us does not make us timid, but
gives us power, love and self-discipline.
—*2 Timothy 1:6–7 NIV*

His divine power has given us
everything required for life
and godliness through the
knowledge of Him who called us
by His own glory and goodness.

—*2 Peter 1:3*

Now I know that the Lord saves his anointed one;
God answers his anointed one
from his heavenly sanctuary,
answering with mighty acts of salvation
achieved by his strong hand.

—*Psalm 20:6* CEB

> He gives strength to the weary
> and strengthens the powerless.
> —*Isaiah 40:29*

For the kingdom of God is not a
matter of talk but of power.
—*1 Corinthians 4:20*

For who is God besides Yahweh?
And who is a rock? Only our God.
God—He clothes me with strength
and makes my way perfect.
He makes my feet like the feet of a deer
and sets me securely on the heights.
—*Psalm 18:31–33*

PROMISES *from* GOD'S HEART
WHEN YOU *pray* ...

Call to Me and I will answer you and tell you great
and incomprehensible things you do not know.
—*Jeremiah 33:3*

But when you pray, go into your most private
room, close the door and pray to your Father
who is in secret, and your Father who sees
[what is done] in secret will reward you.
—*Matthew 6:6* AMP

LORD, the king finds joy in Your strength.
How greatly he rejoices in Your victory!
You have given him his heart's desire
and have not denied the request of his lips. *Selah*
For You meet him with rich blessings;
You place a crown of pure gold on his head.
—*Psalm 21:1–3*

> Confess your sins to each other
> and pray for each other so that you may
> be healed. The prayer of a righteous
> person is powerful and effective.
>
> —*James* 5:16 NIV

"Keep asking, and it will be given to you. Keep searching, and you will find. Keep knocking, and the door will be opened to you. For everyone who asks receives, and the one who searches finds, and to the one who knocks, the door will be opened."

—*Matthew* 7:7–8

> Now if any of you lacks wisdom,
> he should ask God, who gives to all
> generously and without criticizing,
> and it will be given to him.
>
> —*James 1:5*

Depart from me, all you who do iniquity,
For the LORD has heard the voice of my weeping.
The LORD has heard my supplication,
The LORD receives my prayer.
All my enemies will be ashamed
and greatly dismayed;
They shall turn back,
they will suddenly be ashamed.

—*Psalm 6:8–10 NASB*

PROMISES *from* GOD'S HEART FOR HIS *presence* IN YOUR LIFE...

The LORD is in His holy temple;
the LORD's throne is in heaven.
His eyes watch; He examines everyone.
—*Psalm 11:4*

> Draw near to God, and
> He will draw near to you.
> —*James 4:8*

From one man he made all the nations, that they
should inhabit the whole earth; and he marked out
their appointed times in history and the boundaries
of their lands. God did this so that they would
seek him and perhaps reach out for him and find
him, though he is not far from any one of us.
—*Acts 17:26–27 NIV*

But let all who take refuge in You rejoice;
let them shout for joy forever. . . .
For You, LORD, bless the righteous one;
You surround him with favor like a shield.

—*Psalm 5:11–12*

Neither death nor life, neither angels
nor demons, neither the present nor
the future, nor any powers, neither
height nor depth, nor anything
else in all creation, will be able to
separate us from the love of God that
is in Christ Jesus our Lord.

—*Romans 8:38–39 NIV*

"If you love Me, you will keep My commands. And I will ask the Father, and He will give you another Counselor to be with you forever. He is the Spirit of truth. . . . The world . . . doesn't see Him or know Him. But you do know Him, because He remains with you and will be in you."

—*John 14:15–17*

His glory is great through Your victory;
You confer majesty and splendor on him.
You give him blessings forever;
You cheer him with joy in Your presence.
For the king relies on the LORD;
through the faithful love of the Most High
he is not shaken.

—*Psalm 21:5–7*

PROMISES *from* GOD'S HEART
FOR HIS *provision*...

> Young lions lack food and go hungry,
> but those who seek the LORD
> will not lack any good thing.
>
> —*Psalm 34:10*

Bring the full tithe into the storehouse, that there
may be food in my house. And thereby put me to
the test, says the LORD of hosts, if I will not open
the windows of heaven for you and pour down
for you a blessing until there is no more need.

—*Malachi 3:10* ESV

He waters the mountains from His palace . . .
He causes grass to grow for the livestock
and provides crops for man to cultivate,
producing food from the earth . . .
and bread that sustains man's heart.

—*Psalm 104:13–15*

And my God will meet all your
needs according to the riches
of his glory in Christ Jesus.

—*Philippians 4:19 NIV*

The Spirit of the Lord God is upon me . . .
to bring good news to the poor;
he has sent me to bind up the brokenhearted,
to proclaim liberty to the captives,
and the opening of the prison
to those who are bound;
. . . to give them a beautiful headdress
instead of ashes,
the oil of gladness instead of mourning,
the garment of praise instead of a faint spirit;
that they may be called oaks of righteousness,
the planting of the Lord, that he may be glorified.
—*Isaiah 61:1, 3 ESV*

PROMISES *from* GOD'S HEART
FOR YOUR *protection*...

You are being protected by God's
power through faith for a salvation that is
ready to be revealed in the last time.

—*1 Peter 1:5*

God will command his angels
to protect you wherever you go.
—*Psalm 91:11* CEV

A man is a fool to trust himself! But those
who use God's wisdom are safe.

—*Proverbs 30:5*

Hide your loved ones in the shelter
of your presence, safe beneath
your hand, safe from all conspiring
men. Blessed is the Lord, for he has
shown me that his never-failing love
protects me like the walls of a fort!

—*Psalm 31:20–21 TLB*

He will cover you with His feathers;
you will take refuge under His wings.
His faithfulness will be a protective shield.

—*Psalm 91:4*

Now to Him who is able to protect you from stumbling and to make you stand in the presence of His glory, blameless and with great joy, to the only God our Savior, through Jesus Christ our Lord, be glory, majesty, power, and authority before all time, now and forever.

—*Jude 24 NIV*

For the LORD loves justice
and will not abandon His faithful ones.
They are kept safe forever.

—*Psalm 37:28*

A man is a fool to trust himself! But those who use God's wisdom are safe.

—*Proverbs 28:26 TLB*

Promises *from* God's heart for His *purpose* for you...

For I know the plans I have for you," declares the Lord, "plans to prosper you and not to harm you, plans to give you hope and a future.
—*Jeremiah 29:11 NIV*

And we know that all things work together for good for those who love God, who are called according to his purpose, because those whom he foreknew he also predestined to be conformed to the image of his Son, that his Son would be the firstborn among many brothers and sisters.
—*Romans 8:28–29 NET*

> "Follow Me," He told them, "and I will make you fish for people!"
> —*Matthew 4:19*

God has given us this task of reconciling people to him. For God was in Christ, reconciling the world to himself, no longer counting people's sins against them. And he gave us this wonderful message of reconciliation.

—*2 Corinthians 5:18–19* NLT

He said to him, "Love the Lord your God with all your heart, with all your soul, and with all your mind. This is the greatest and most important[c] command. The second is like it: Love your neighbor as yourself. All the Law and the Prophets depend on these two commands."

—*Matthew 22:37–40*

> You yourselves, as living stones, are being built into a spiritual house for a holy priesthood to offer spiritual sacrifices acceptable to God through Jesus Christ.
>
> —1 Peter 2:5

One thing I [Paul] do: Forgetting what is behind and reaching forward to what is ahead, I pursue as my goal the prize promised by God's heavenly call in Christ Jesus. . . . Our citizenship is in heaven, from which we also eagerly wait for a Savior, the Lord Jesus Christ. He will transform the body of our humble condition into the likeness of His glorious body, by the power that enables Him to subject everything to Himself.

—*Philippians 3:13–14, 20–21*

Promises *from* God's heart for *rest and renewal*...

Those who trust in the Lord will renew their
strength; they will soar on wings like eagles; they will
run and not grow weary; they will walk and not faint.

—*Isaiah 40:31*

[The Lord] lets me rest in the meadow grass and
leads me beside the quiet streams. He gives me new
strength. He helps me do what honors him the most.

—*Psalm 23:2–3* TLB

"Come to Me, all of you who are weary
and burdened, and I will give you rest."

—*Matthew 11:28*

That's why we are not discouraged. No, even
if outwardly we are wearing out, inwardly we
are being renewed each and every day.

—*2 Corinthians 4:16 ISV*

The law of the LORD is perfect, restoring
the soul; The testimony of the LORD is
sure, making wise the simple.

—*Psalm 19:7 NASB*

You took off your former way of life, the old
self that is corrupted by deceitful desires; you are
being renewed in the spirit of your minds; you put
on the new self, the one created according to God's
likeness in righteousness and purity of the truth.

—*Ephesians 4:22–23*

Take my yoke upon you, and learn from
me, for I am gentle and lowly in heart,
and you will find rest for your souls.

—*Matthew* 11:29 ESV

He redeems your life from the Pit;
He crowns you with faithful love and compassion.
He satisfies you with goodness;
your youth is renewed like the eagle.

—*Psalm* 103:4–6

Do not be conformed to this world,
but be transformed by the renewal of
your mind, that by testing you may
discern what is the will of God, what
is good and acceptable and perfect.

—*Romans* 12:2 ESV

PROMISES *from* GOD'S HEART
FOR *self-control* ...

Everyone who competes exercises self-
control in everything. However, they do it
to receive a crown that will fade away, but
we a crown that will never fade away.

—*1 Corinthians 9:25*

His divine power has given us everything required
for life and godliness through the knowledge of Him
who called us by His own glory and goodness. ...
For this very reason, make every effort to
supplement your faith with goodness, goodness with
knowledge, knowledge with self-control, self-control
with endurance, endurance with godliness, godliness
with brotherly affection, and brotherly affection
with love. For if these qualities are yours and are
increasing, they will keep you from being useless or
unfruitful in the knowledge of our Lord Jesus Christ.

—*2 Peter 1:3, 5–8*

For freedom Christ has set us free.
Stand firm, then, and do not be subject
again to the yoke of slavery.

—*Galatians 5:1* NET

Lord, who can dwell in Your
tent? Who can live on Your holy
mountain? The one who lives
honestly, practices righteousness, and
acknowledges the truth in his heart.

—*Psalm 15:1–2*

> God didn't give us a spirit that is
> timid but one that is powerful,
> loving, and self-controlled.
> —2 Timothy 1:7 CEB

The LORD is good and upright;
therefore He shows sinners the way.
He leads the humble in what is right
and teaches them His way.
All the LORD's ways show faithful love and truth
to those who keep His covenant and decrees.
—Psalm 25:8–10

Promises *from* God's heart for *spiritual gifts...*

God also testified by signs and wonders,
various miracles, and distributions of gifts
from the Holy Spirit according to His will.
—*Hebrews 2:4*

> But the fruit that the Spirit
> produces in a person's life is love,
> joy, peace, patience, kindness,
> goodness, faithfulness,
> —*Galatians 5:22 ERV*

You yourselves, as living stones, are being built into a
spiritual house for a holy priesthood to offer spiritual
sacrifices acceptable to God through Jesus Christ.
—*1 Peter 2:5*

> See, the Lord God comes with strength,
> and His power establishes His rule.
> His reward is with Him,
> and His gifts accompany Him.
>
> —*Isaiah 40:9–11*

Now as we have many parts in one body, and all the parts do not have the same function, in the same way we who are many are one body in Christ and individually members of one another. According to the grace given to us, we have different gifts: If prophecy, use it according to the standard of one's faith; if service, in service; if teaching, in teaching; if exhorting, in exhortation; giving, with generosity; leading, with diligence; showing mercy, with cheerfulness.

—*Romans 12:4–8*

Let love be your greatest aim; nevertheless,
ask also for the special abilities the Holy Spirit
gives, and especially the gift of prophecy,
being able to preach the messages of God.
But if your gift is that of being able to "speak in
tongues," that is, to speak in languages you haven't
learned, you will be talking to God but not to others,
since they won't be able to understand you. You will
be speaking by the power of the Spirit, but it will
all be a secret. But one who prophesies, preaching
the messages of God, is helping others grow in
the Lord, encouraging and comforting them.

—*1 Corinthians 14:1–3* TLB

Promises *from* God's heart
for when you *stray*...

"If a man has a hundred sheep, and one wanders
away and is lost, what will he do? Won't he
leave the ninety-nine others and go out into
the hills to search for the lost one? And if he
finds it, he will rejoice over it more than over
the ninety-nine others safe at home!"

—*Matthew* 18:12–13 *TLB*

"Or what woman who has 10 silver coins, if she
loses one coin, does not light a lamp, sweep
the house, and search carefully until she finds
it? When she finds it, she calls her women friends
and neighbors together, saying, 'Rejoice with me,
because I have found the silver coin I lost!'"

—*Luke* 15:8–9

The one who conceals his sins will not
prosper, but whoever confesses and
renounces them will find mercy.
—*Proverbs 28:13*

We have redemption,
the forgiveness of sins, in Him.
—*Colossians 1:14*

But go and learn what this means: 'I desire mercy
and not sacrifice.' For I did not come to call
the righteous, but sinners, to repentance."
—*Matthew 9:13* NKJV

"But his father said to the servants, 'Quick! Bring the finest robe in the house and put it on him. Get a ring for his finger and sandals for his feet. And kill the calf we have been fattening. We must celebrate with a feast, for this son of mine was dead and has now returned to life. He was lost, but now he is found.' So the party began."

—*Luke 15:22–24* NLT

If you return, I will restore you; you will stand in My presence.

—*Jeremiah 15:19*

For the Son of Man has come to save that which was lost.

—*Matthew 18:11* NKJV

Promises *from* God's heart
when you need *strength* . . .

He gives strength to the weary
and strengthens the powerless.
—*Isaiah 40:29*

The LORD is the strength of His people;
He is a stronghold of salvation
for His anointed.
—*Psalm 28:8*

See, the Lord God comes with strength,
and His power establishes His rule. . . .
He protects His flock like a shepherd;
He gathers the lambs in His arms
and carries them in the fold of His garment.
—*Isaiah 40:10–11*

He makes both us and you remain strong in the faith because we belong to Christ. He anointed us.

—*2 Corinthians 1:21 NIRV*

Those who trust in the LORD
will renew their strength;
they will soar on wings like eagles;
they will run and not grow weary;
they will walk and not faint.

—*Isaiah 40:31*

I pray that the eyes of your heart will have enough light to see what is the hope of God's call, what is the richness of God's glorious inheritance among believers, and what is the overwhelming greatness of God's power that is working among us believers. This power is conferred by the energy of God's powerful strength.

—*Ephesians 1:18–19 CEB*

But all those who come and listen and obey me are like a man who builds a house on a strong foundation laid upon the underlying rock. When the floodwaters rise and break against the house, it stands firm, for it is strongly built.

—*Luke 6:47–48 TLB*

Promises *from* God's heart when facing *trials*...

Though now for a short time you have had to struggle in various trials so that the genuineness of your faith—more valuable than gold, which perishes though refined by fire—may result in praise, glory, and honor at the revelation of Jesus Christ.

—*1 Peter 1:6–8*

Consider it a great joy, my brothers, whenever you experience various trials, knowing that the testing of your faith produces endurance. But endurance must do its complete work, so that you may be mature and complete, lacking nothing.

—*James 1:2–4*

Fear not, for I am with you;
be not dismayed, for I am your God;
I will strengthen you, I will help you,
I will uphold you with my righteous right hand.

—*Isaiah 41:10* ESV

God will bless you, if you don't give up
when your faith is being tested. He will
reward you with a glorious life, just as he
rewards everyone who loves him.

—*James 1:12* CEV

May the Lord be praised!
Day after day He bears our burdens;
God is our salvation.

—*Psalm 68:19*

> Stoop down and reach out to those
> who are oppressed. Share their
> burdens, and so complete Christ's law.
> —*Galatians 6:2* THE MESSAGE

Your promise revives me;
it comforts me in all my troubles.
The proud hold me in utter contempt,
but I do not turn away from your instructions.
I meditate on your age-old regulations;
O Lord, they comfort me.

—*Psalm* 119:50, 52 NLT

For our momentary light affliction
is producing for us an absolutely
incomparable eternal weight of glory.

—*2 Corinthians* 4:17

PROMISES *from* GOD'S HEART
FOR HIS *truth* ...

> "You will know the truth, and
> the truth will set you free."
> —*John 8:32*

The sum of your word is truth,
and every one of your righteous
rules endures forever.
—*Psalm 119:160 ESV*

This is what the LORD says—
your Redeemer, the Holy One of Israel:
"I am the LORD your God,
who teaches you what is best for you,
who directs you in the way you should go."
—*Isaiah 48:17 NIV*

I have hidden your word in my heart
that I might not sin against you.
Praise be to you, LORD.

—*Psalm 119:11–12*

God! His way is perfect;
the LORD's word is tried and true.
He is a shield for all who
take refuge in him.

—*Psalm 18:30 CEB*

"Therefore everyone who hears these words of
mine and puts them into practice is like a wise
man who built his house on the rock. The rain
came down, the streams rose, and the winds blew
and beat against that house; yet it did not fall,
because it had its foundation on the rock."

—*Matthew 7:24–25 NIV*

> Truthful lips will be established forever,
> But a lying tongue is [credited]
> only for a moment.
> —*Proverbs 12:19* AMP

When you heard the message of truth, the
gospel of your salvation, and when you
believed in Him, you were also sealed with
the promised Holy Spirit. He is the down
payment of our inheritance, for the redemption
of the possession, to the praise of His glory.
—*Ephesians 1:13–14*

By His own choice, He gave us a new birth
by the message of truth so that we would
be the firstfruits of His creatures.
—*James 1:18*

PROMISES *from* GOD'S HEART
FOR HIS *victory*...

Now I know that the LORD gives victory to His
anointed; He will answer him from His holy heaven
with mighty victories from His right hand.

—Psalm 20:6

I put no trust in my bow,
my sword does not bring me victory;
but you give us victory over our enemies,
you put our adversaries to shame.
In God we make our boast all day long,
and we will praise your name forever.

—Psalm 44:6–8 NIV

A horse is prepared for the
day of battle, but victory
comes from the LORD.

—Proverbs 21:31

The sting of death is sin, and the power of sin
is the law. But thanks be to God! He gives us
the victory through our Lord Jesus Christ.

—*1 Corinthians 15:56–57 NIV*

Whatever has been born of
God conquers the world. This is
the victory that has conquered
the world: our faith.

—*1 John 5:4*

The righteous man will be remembered forever.
He will not fear bad news;
his heart is confident, trusting in the LORD.
His heart is assured; he will not fear.
In the end he will look in triumph on his foes.

—*Psalm 112:6–8*

The Lord is on my side; I will not fear.
What can man do to me?
The Lord is on my side as my helper;
I shall look in triumph on those who hate me.
—*Psalm* 118:6–7 ESV

Therefore, since we have been
declared righteous by faith, we have
peace with God through our Lord
Jesus Christ. We have also obtained
access through Him by faith into this
grace in which we stand, and we rejoice
in the hope of the glory of God.
—*Romans* 5:1–2

PROMISES *from* GOD'S HEART WHEN YOU ARE *weak and weary*...

"Come to Me, all of you who are weary and burdened, and I will give you rest. All of you, take up My yoke and learn from Me, because I am gentle and humble in heart, and you will find rest for yourselves."

—*Matthew 11:28–29*

Remember Your word to Your servant;
You have given me hope through it.
This is my comfort in my affliction:
Your promise has given me life.

—*Psalm 119:49–50*

I keep the LORD in mind always.
Because He is at my right hand,
I will not be shaken.
Therefore my heart is glad
and my spirit rejoices;
my body also rests securely.

—*Psalm 16:8–9*

"My grace is sufficient for you, for power is perfected
in weakness." Therefore, I [Paul] will most
gladly boast all the more about my weaknesses,
so that Christ's power may reside in me.

—*2 Corinthians 12:1*

For the moment all discipline seems painful rather than pleasant, but later it yields the peaceful fruit of righteousness to those who have been trained by it. Therefore lift your drooping hands and strengthen your weak knees, and make straight paths for your feet, so that what is lame may not be put out of joint but rather be healed.

—*Hebrews 12:11–13 ESV*

So let's not get tired of doing what is good. At just the right time we will reap a harvest of blessing if we don't give up.

—*Galatians 6:9 NLT*

Promises *from* God's heart when you are *worried*...

"Don't worry about your life, what you will eat or what you will drink; or about your body, what you will wear. Isn't life more than food and the body more than clothing? Look at the birds of the sky: They don't sow or reap or gather into barns, yet your heavenly Father feeds them. Aren't you worth more than they?"

—*Matthew 6:25–26*

The Lord is my strength and shield. I trust him with all my heart. He helps me, and my heart is filled with joy.

—*Psalm 28:7–8 NLT*

Do not be anxious about anything, but
in everything by prayer and
supplication with thanksgiving let
your requests be made known to God.
And the peace of God, which surpasses
all understanding, will guard your hearts
and your minds in Christ Jesus.

—*Philippians 4:6–7* ESV

In God I trust; I will not fear.
What can man do to me?

—*Psalm 56:11*

I will be glad and rejoice in your love,
for you saw my affliction and knew the
anguish of my soul. You have not given
me into the hands of the enemy but
have set my feet in a spacious place.

—*Psalm 31:7–8* NIV

Trust in the LORD with all your heart, and
do not rely on your own understanding;
think about Him in all your ways, and
He will guide you on the right paths.

—*Proverbs 3:5–6*

"Your heart must not
be troubled. Believe in
God; believe also in Me."

—*John 14:1*

He will make your being right and good show as
the light, and your wise actions as the noon day.
Rest in the Lord and be willing to wait for Him.
Do not trouble yourself when all goes well with
the one who carries out his sinful plans. Stop
being angry. Turn away from fighting. Do not
trouble yourself. It leads only to wrong-doing.

—*Psalm 37:6–8* NLV

PROMISES *from* GOD'S HEART
FOR HIS *wisdom*...

If any of you lacks wisdom, you should ask
God, who gives generously to all without
finding fault, and it will be given to you.

—James 1:5 NIV

To obey the LORD is the fundamental principle for
wise living; all who carry out his precepts acquire
good moral insight. He will receive praise forever.

—Psalm 111:10 NET

For the LORD gives wisdom;
from His mouth come knowledge
and understanding.
He stores up success for the upright;
He is a shield for those who live with integrity
so that He may guard the paths of justice
and protect the way of His loyal followers.

—Proverbs 2:6–8

Because of God you are in Christ Jesus, who
has become for us wisdom from God. In Christ
we are put right with God, and have been
made holy, and have been set free from sin.

—*1 Corinthians 1:30 NCV*

How wonderful to be wise, to
understand things, to be able
to analyze them and interpret
them. Wisdom lights up a man's
face, softening its hardness.

—*Ecclesiastes 8:1 TLB*

We have redemption in Him through His blood,
the forgiveness of our trespasses, according
to the riches of His grace that He lavished on
us with all wisdom and understanding.

—*Ephesians 1:7–8*

This also comes
from the LORD of Hosts.
He gives wonderful advice;
He gives great wisdom.
—*Isaiah 28:29*

All the treasures of wisdom and
knowledge are hidden in Him.
—*Colossians 2:3*

For to the man who is pleasing in His sight,
He gives wisdom, knowledge, and joy.
—*Ecclesiastes 2:26*

LIVE YOUR FAITH

Dear Friend,

This book was prayerfully crafted with you, the reader, in mind—every word, every sentence, every page—was thoughtfully written, designed, and packaged to encourage you...right where you are this very moment. At DaySpring, our vision is to see every person experience the life-changing message of God's love. So, as we worked through rough drafts, design changes, edits and details, we prayed for you to deeply experience His unfailing love, indescribable peace, and pure joy. It is our sincere hope that through these Truth-filled pages your heart will be blessed, knowing that God cares about you—your desires and disappointments, your challenges and dreams.

He knows. He cares. He loves you unconditionally.

BLESSINGS!
THE DAYSPRING BOOK TEAM

Additional copies of this book and other DaySpring titles can be purchased at fine bookstores everywhere.
Order online at dayspring.com
or
by phone at 1-877-751-4347